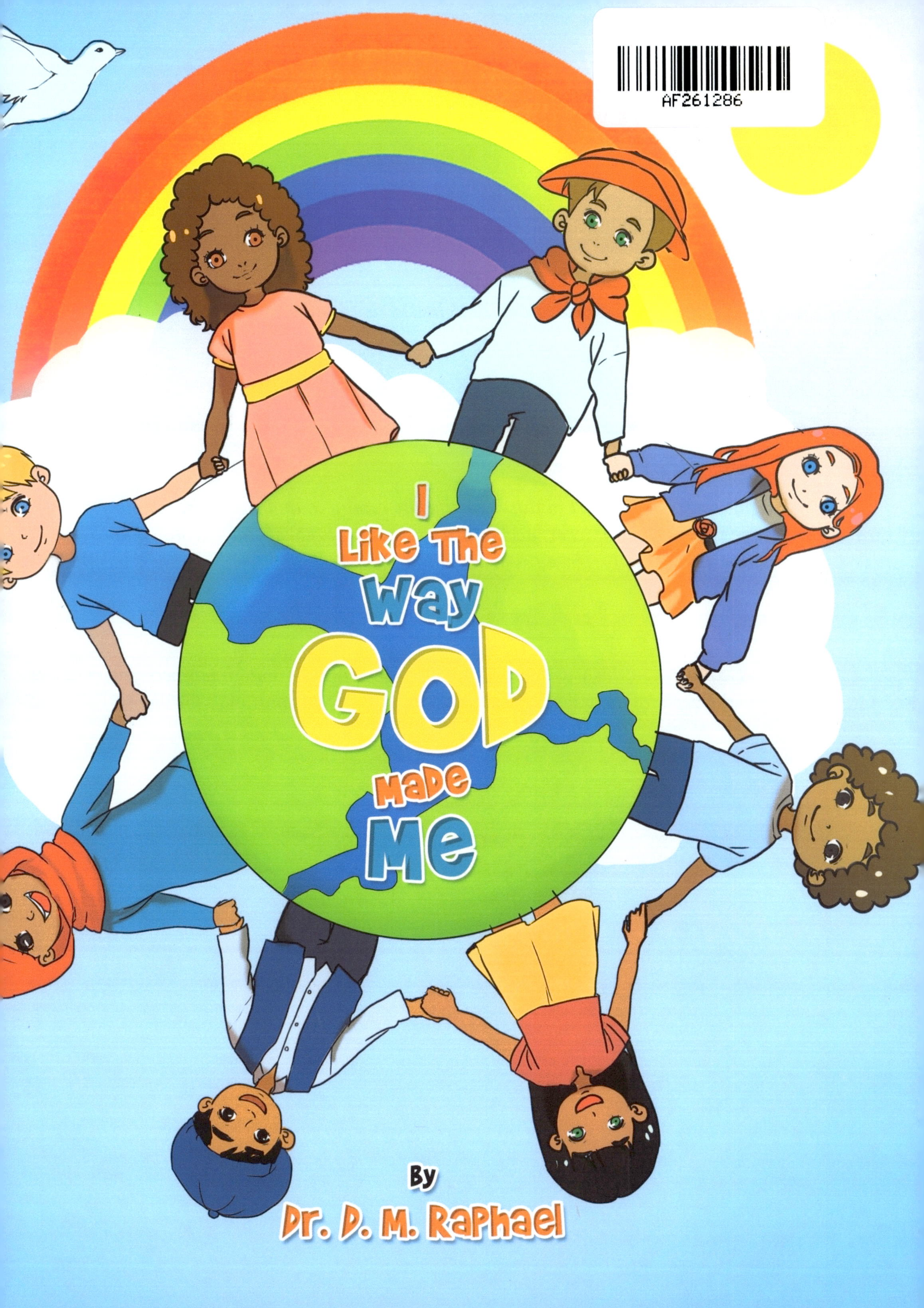

AF261286
I
Like The
Way
GOD
Made
Me
By
Dr. D. M. Raphael

Dedicated to God and my son Christion
You are fearfully and wonderfully made….
Psalm 139:14 KJV

This creative tool allows for adults and children to have an interactive experience with the Word of God. The book encourages children to implement organizational skills using facial features. Please read the words and the scriptures to your child (ren). Allow the child (ren) to point to or identify their facial features and the features of others. When you have finished reading the pages of the book, cut the facial features out in the back of the book and create faces in the book or a separate sheet of paper using glue, tape, or paste. Teach your child (ren) about how much God loves them and that they were uniquely and wonderfully made in His image.

I like the way God made my hair.

But the very hairs of your head are all numbered.
Matthew 10:30 KVJ

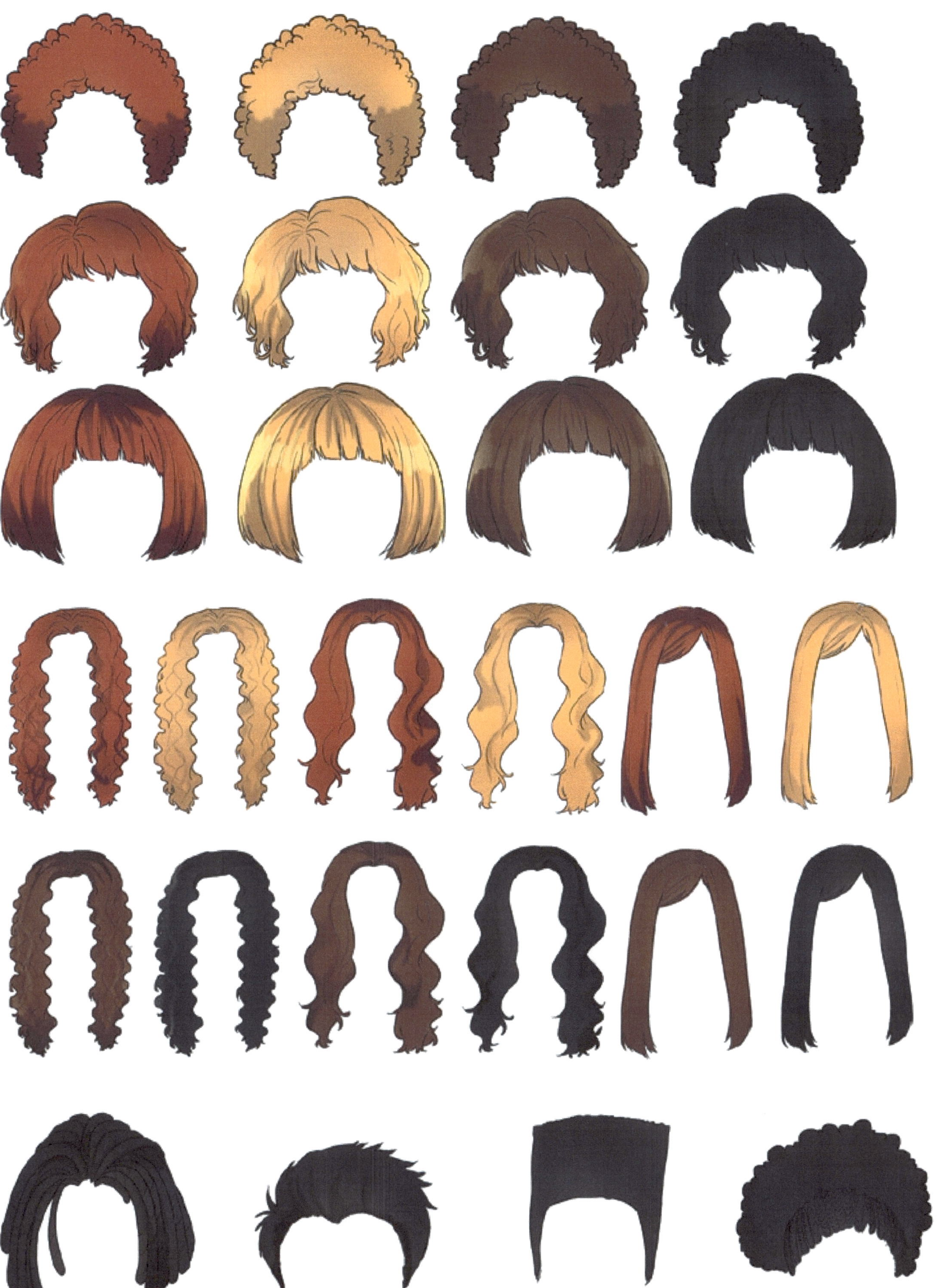

I like the way God made my eyes.

Keep me as the apple of your eye;
hide me in the shadow of your wings
Psalm 17:8 NIV

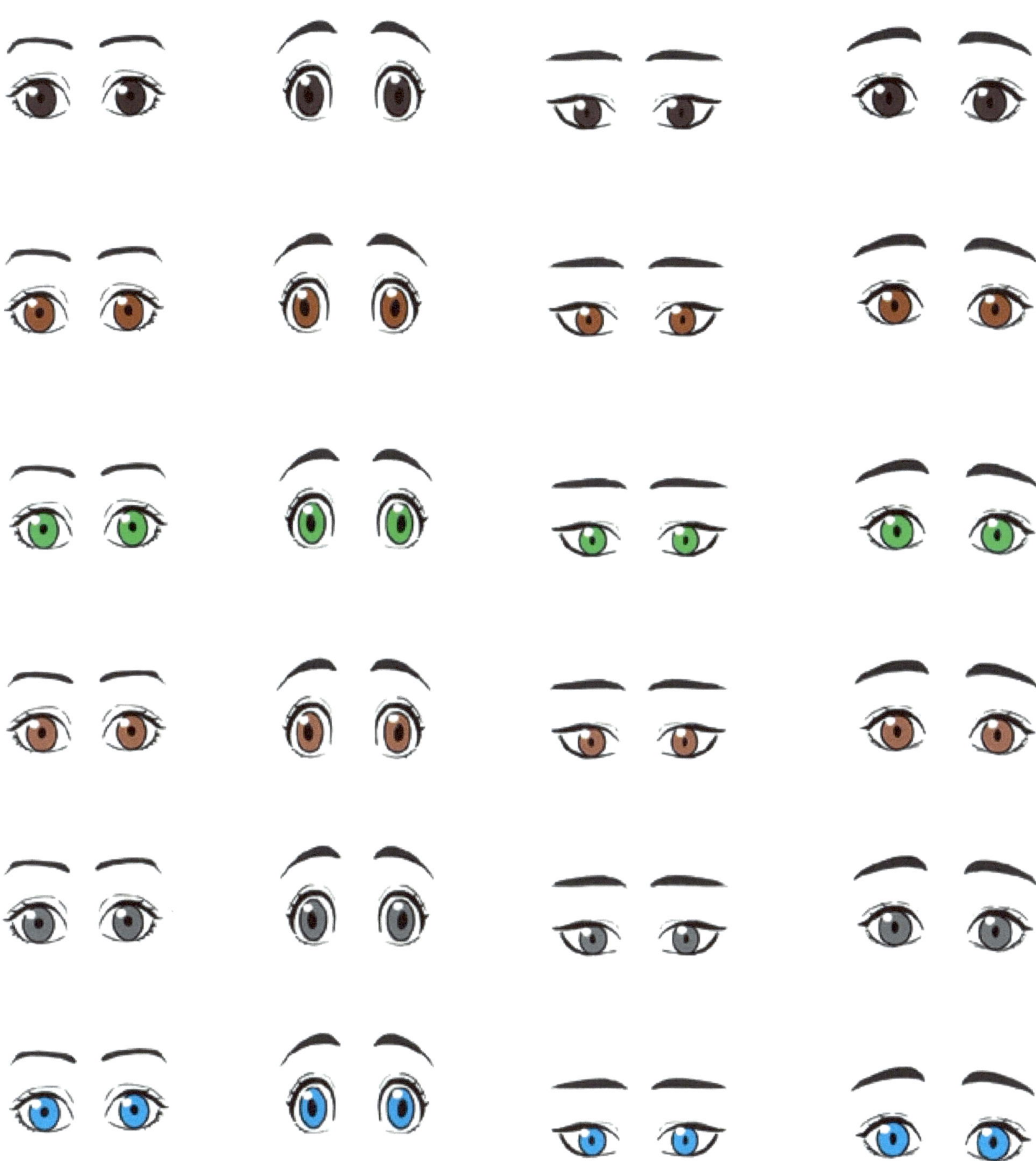

I like the way God made my ears.

Make your ear attentive to wisdom, incline
your heart to understanding.
Proverbs 2:2 NASB

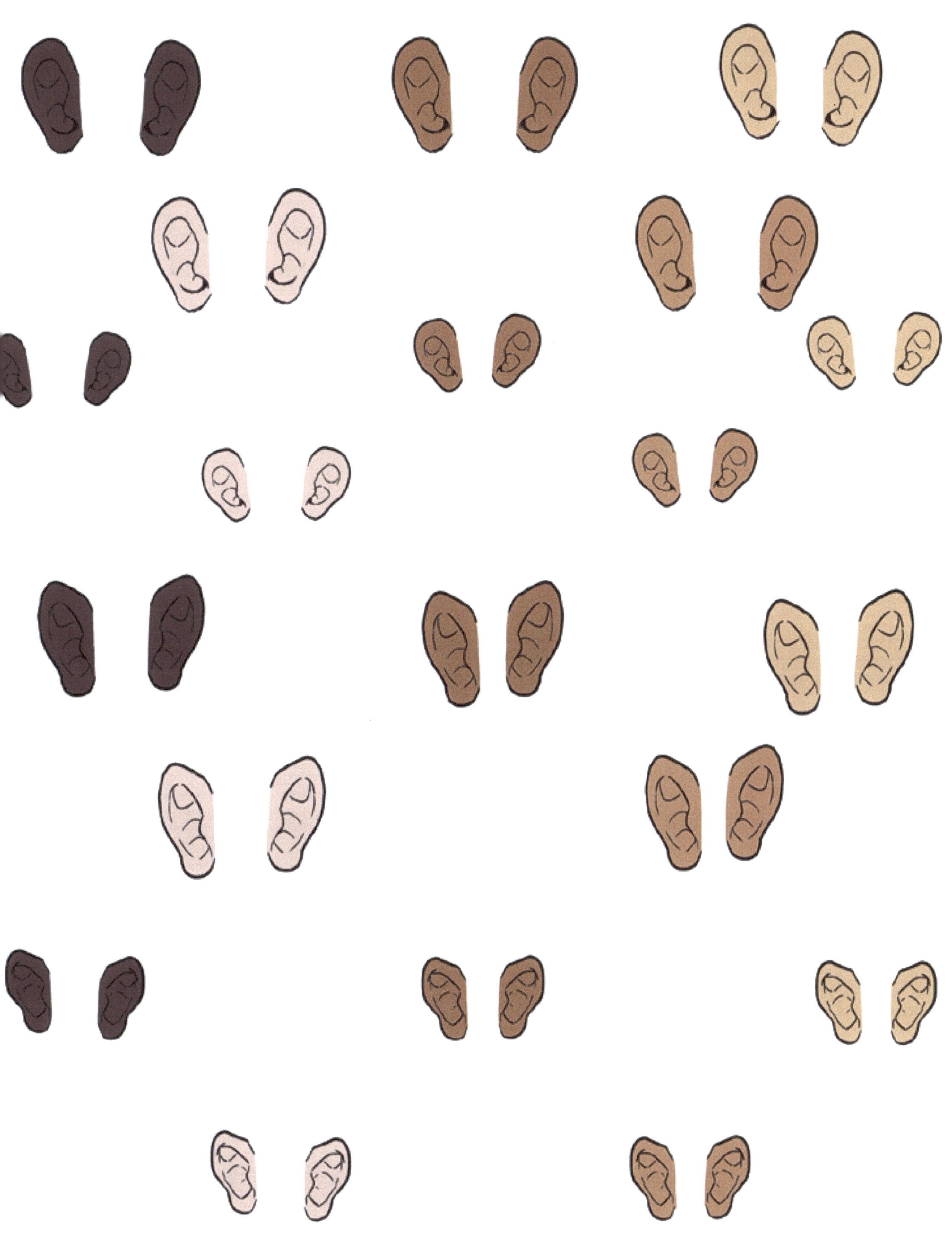

I like the way God made my nose.

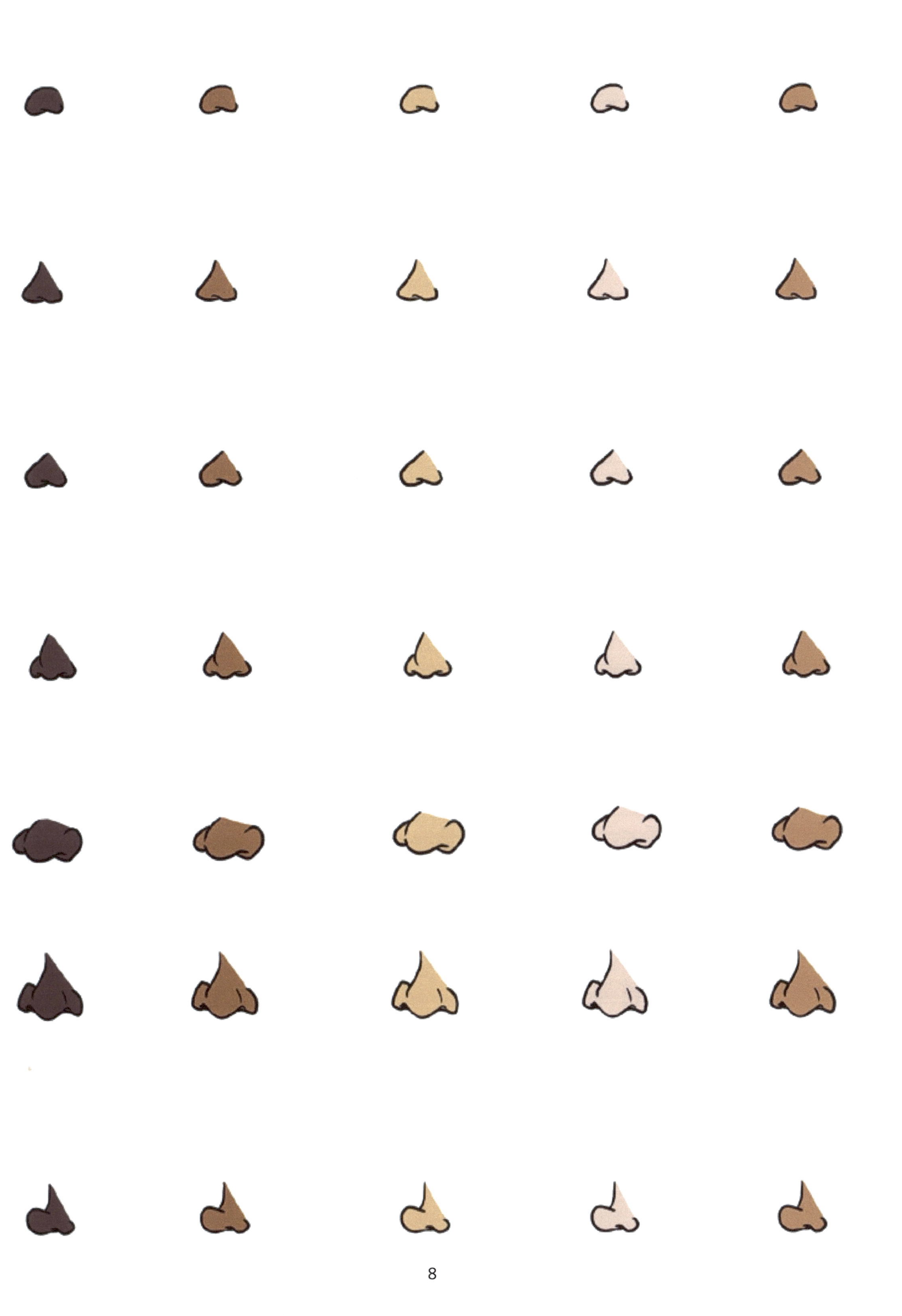

I like the way God made my mouth.

Let the words of my mouth and the meditation
of my heart Be acceptable in Your sight O Lord,
my rock and my Redeemer
Psalms 19:14 NASB 1995

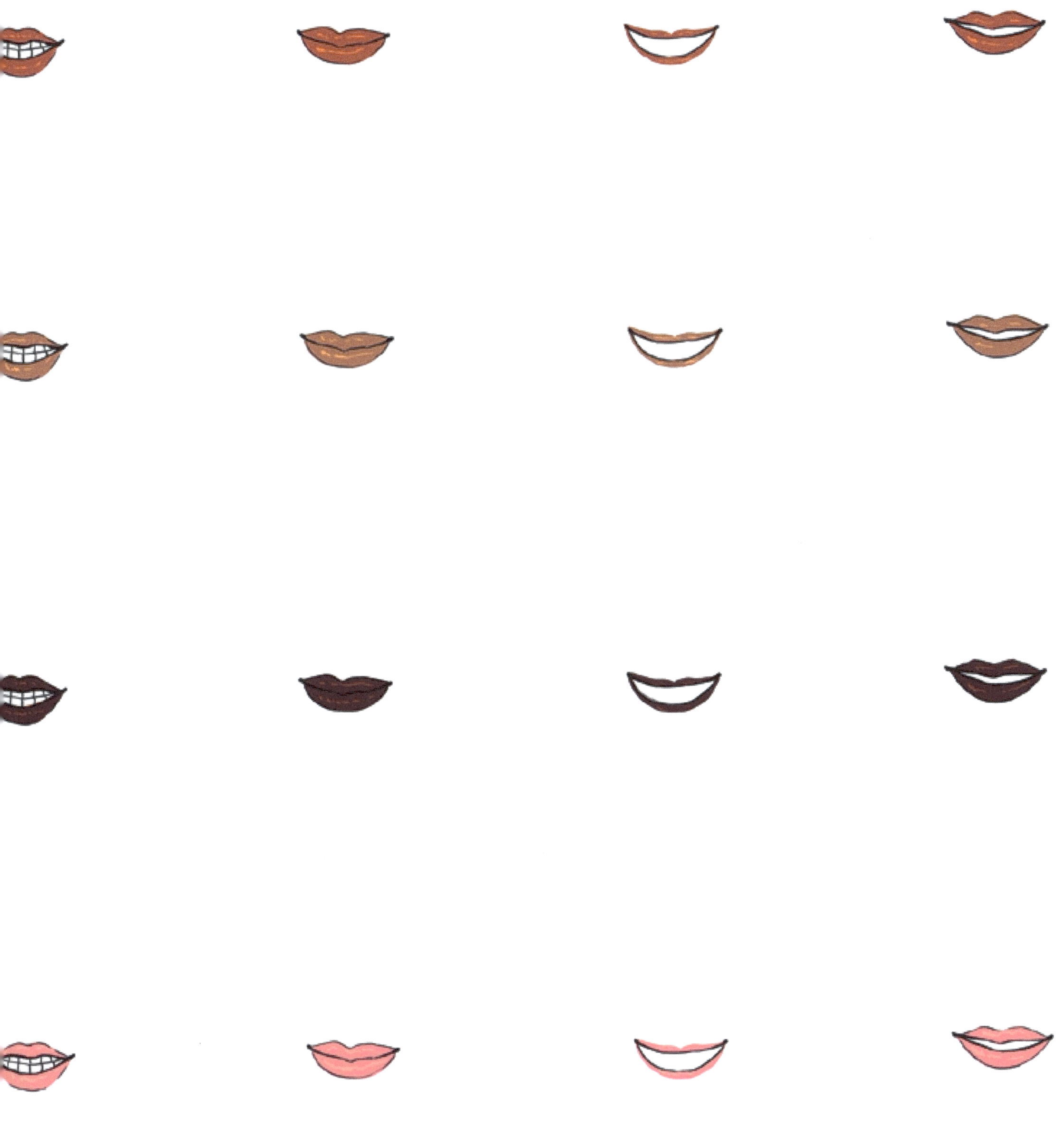

I like the way God made me.

I will give thanks to You, for I am fearfully and wonderfully made;
Wonderful are Your works, And my soul knows it very well.
Psalm 139:14 NASB 1995

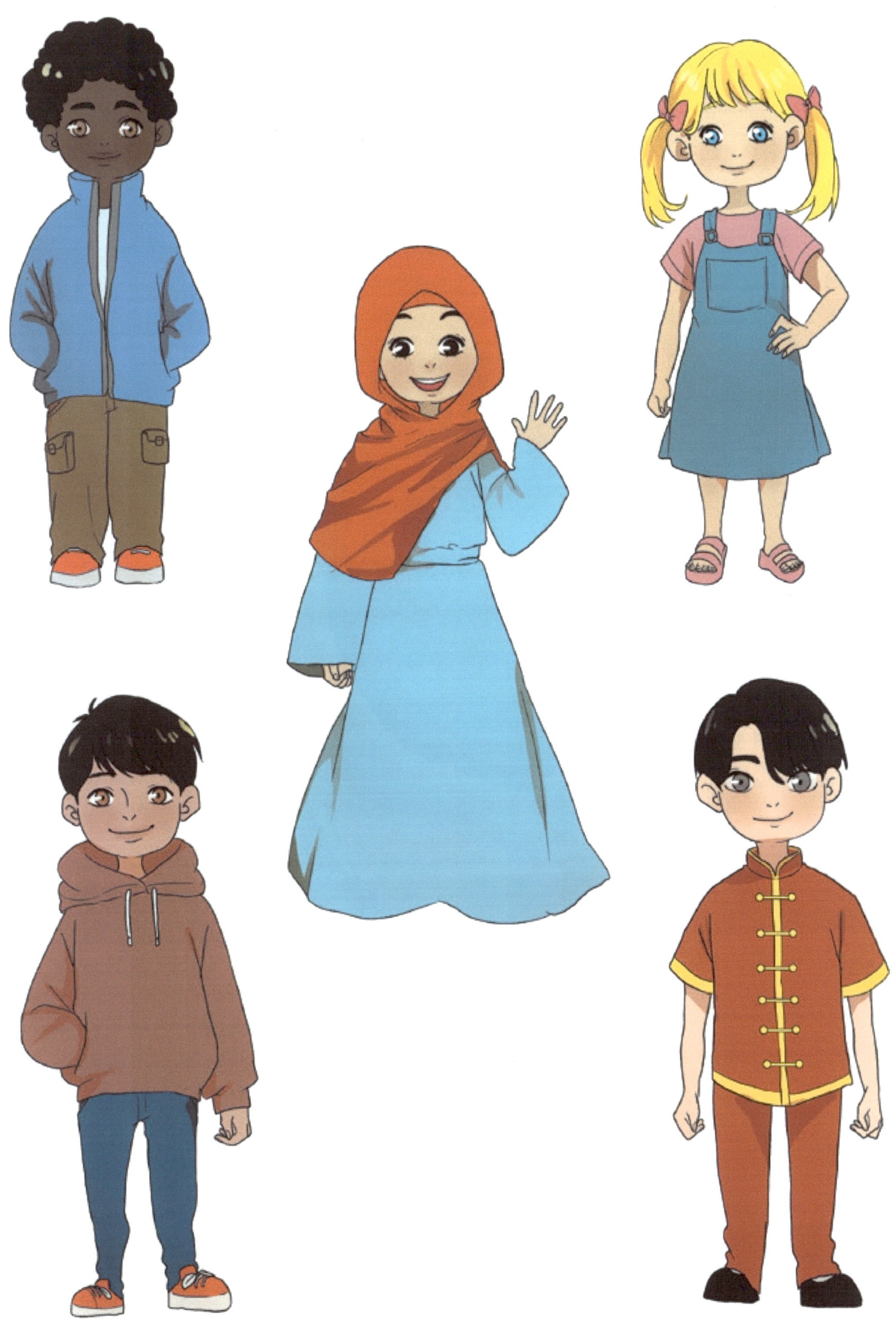

Create Your Face

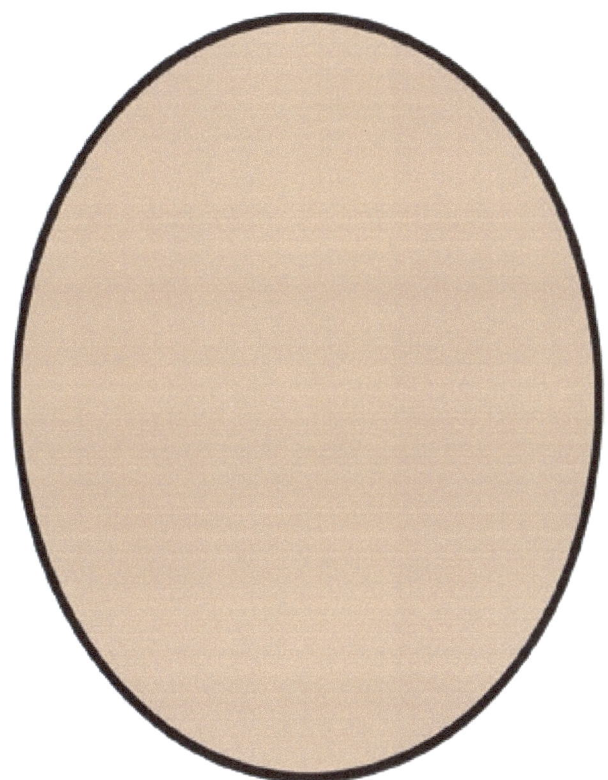

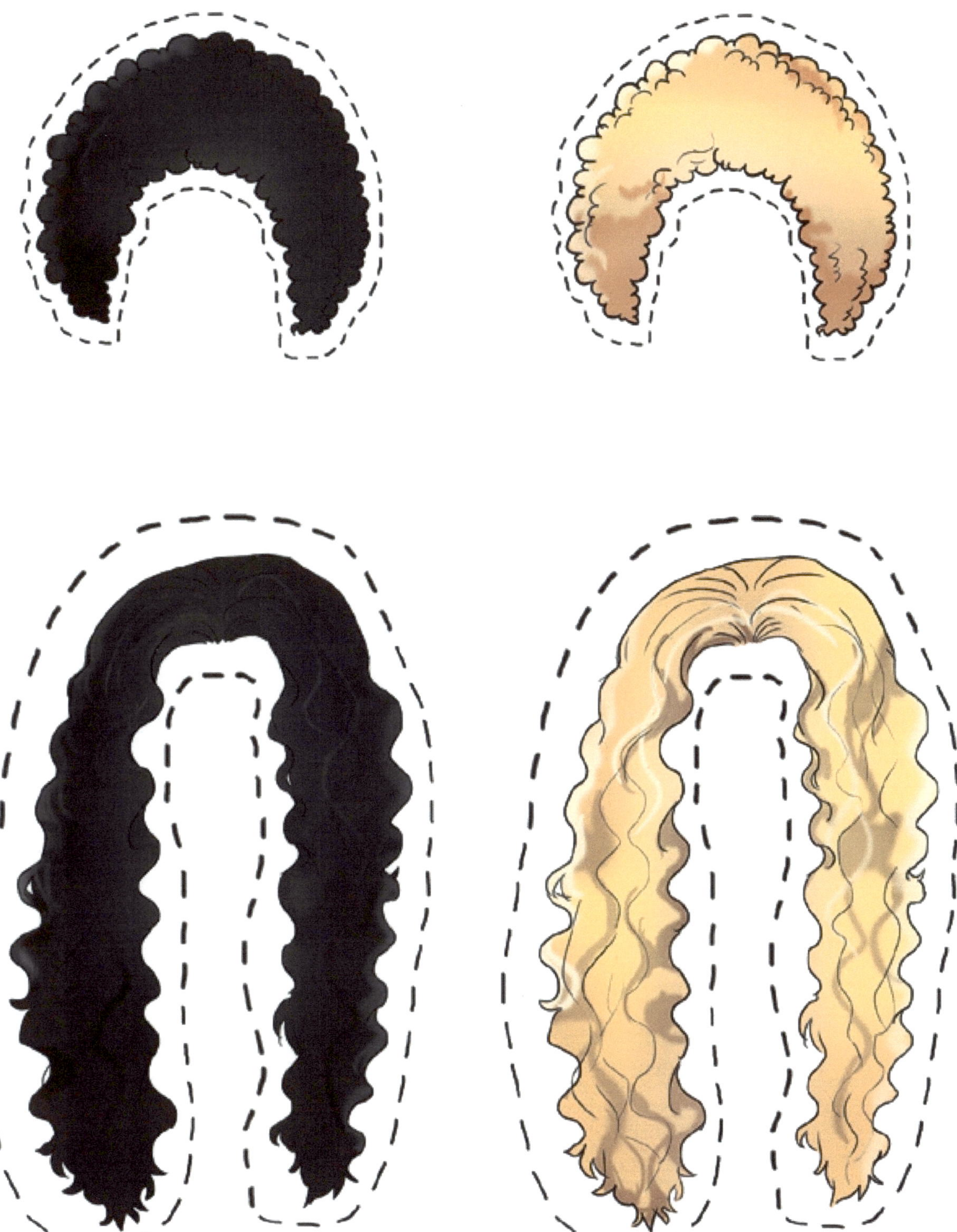

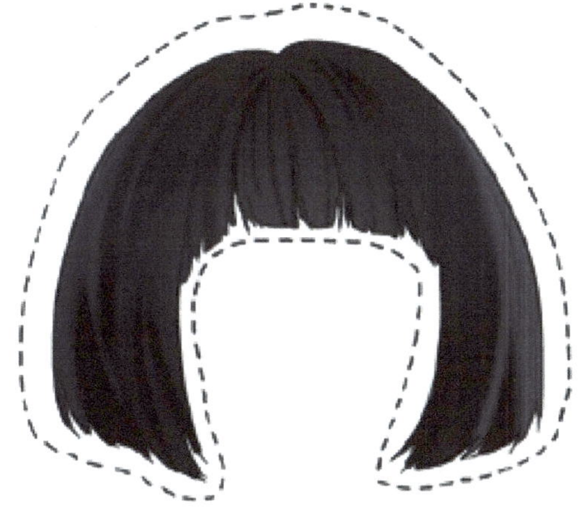

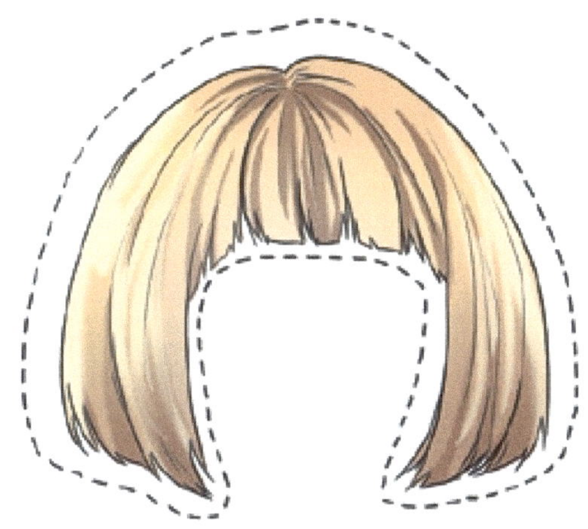

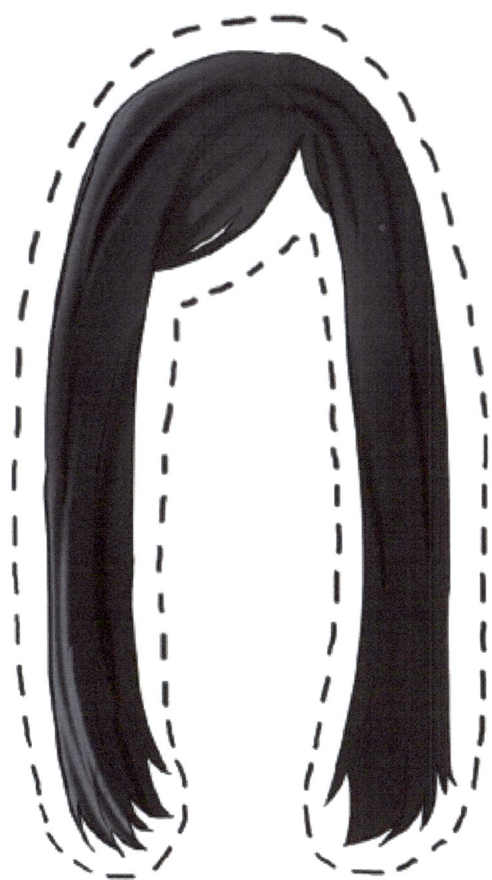

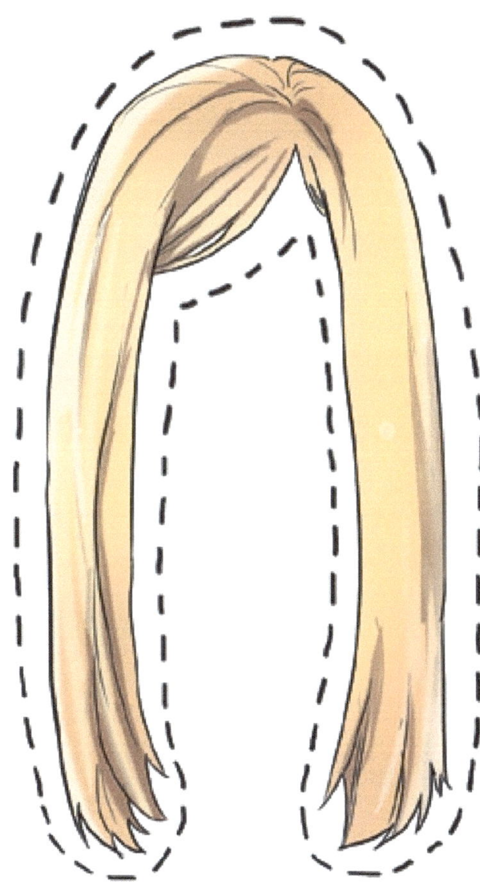

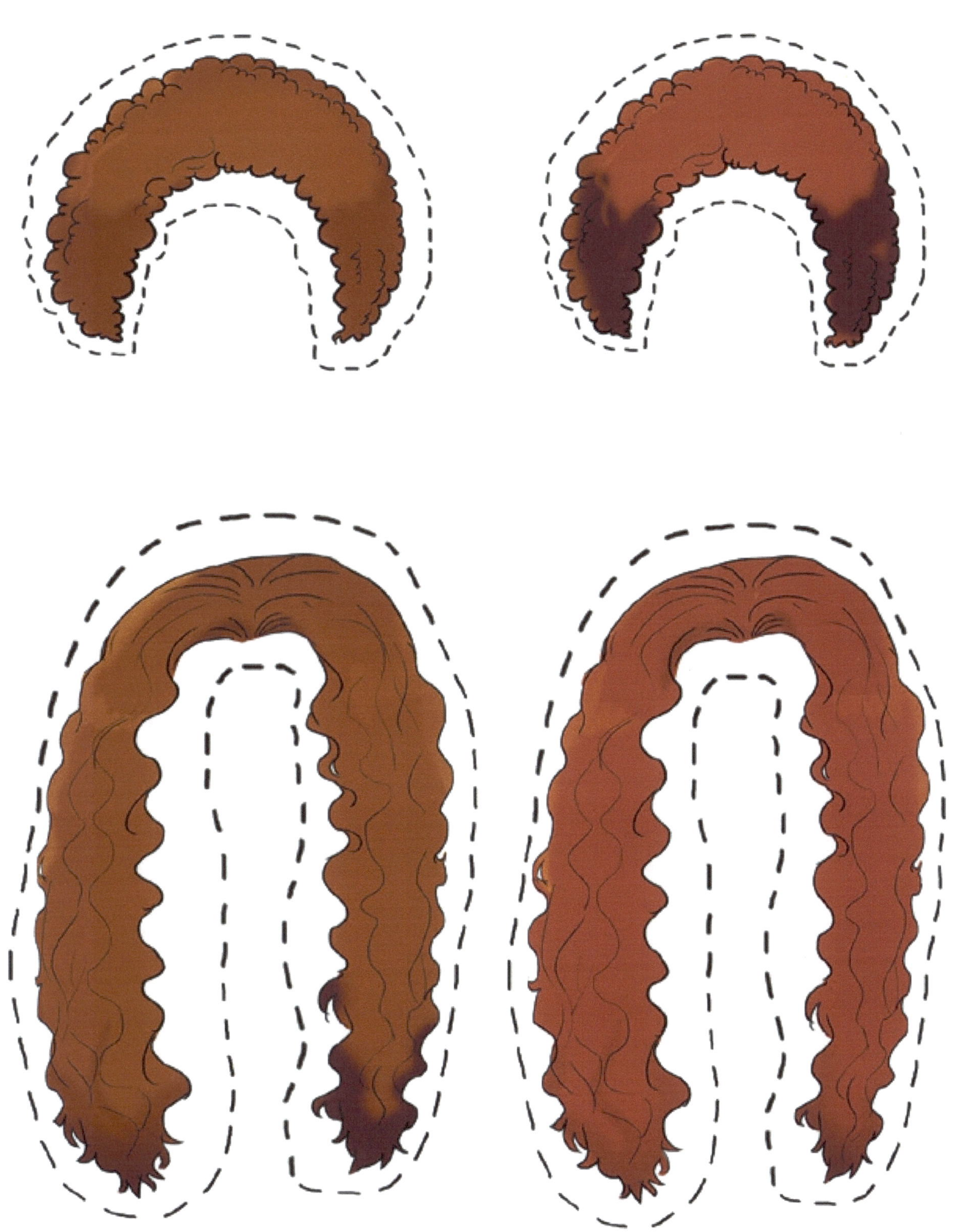

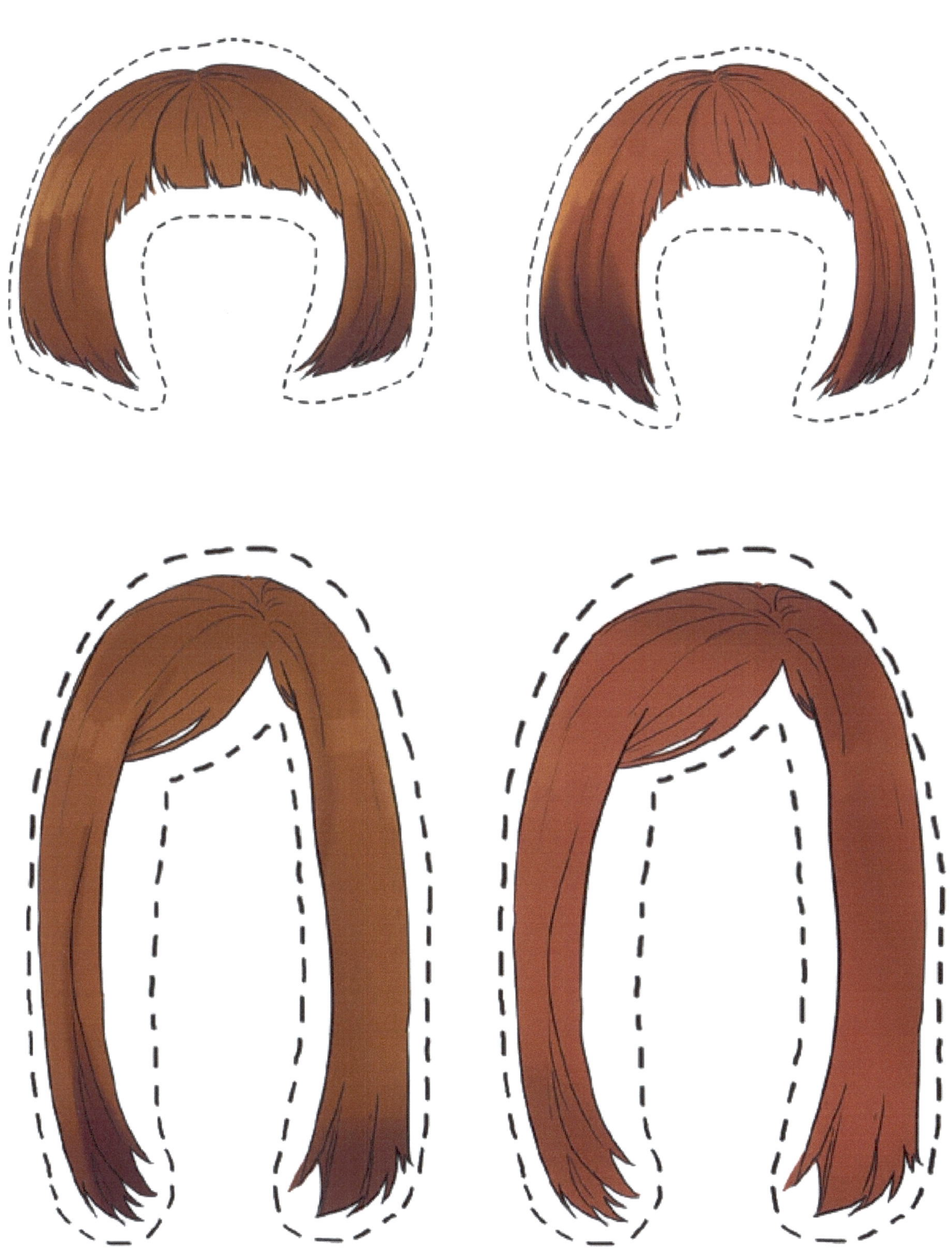

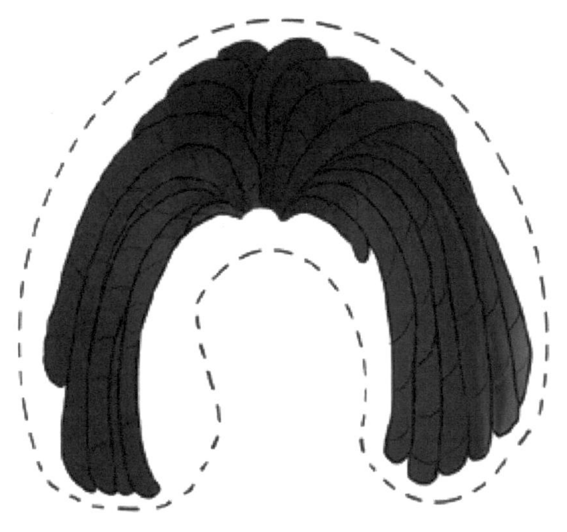
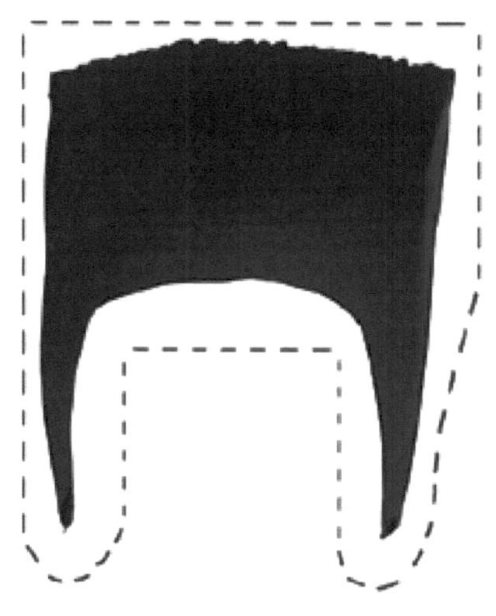
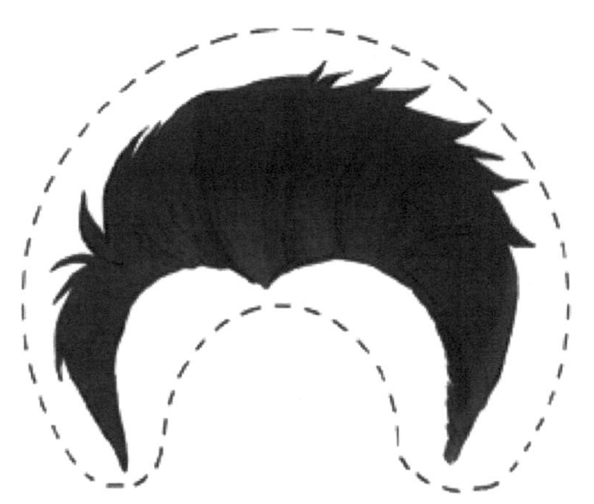
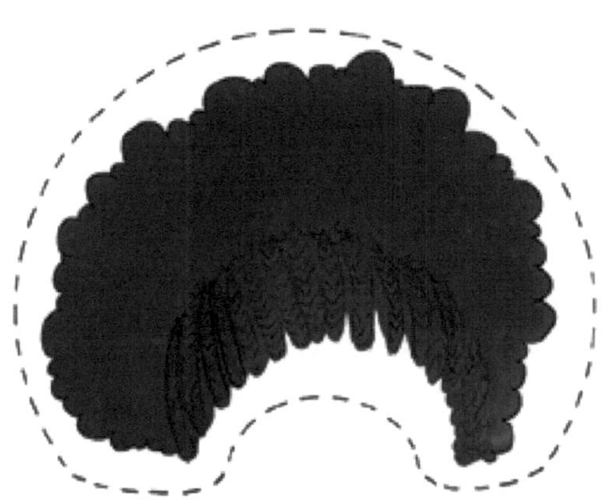

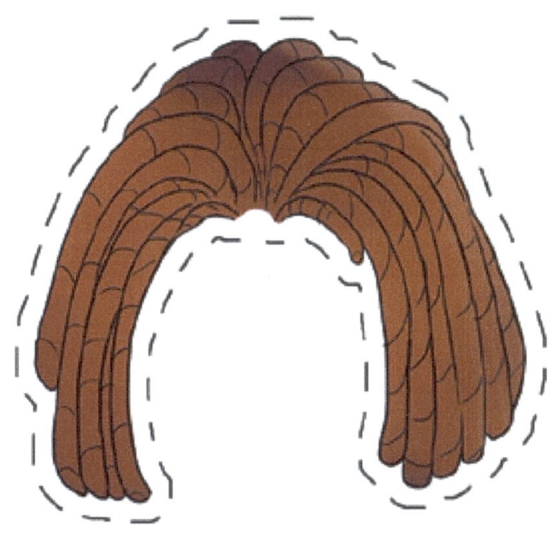

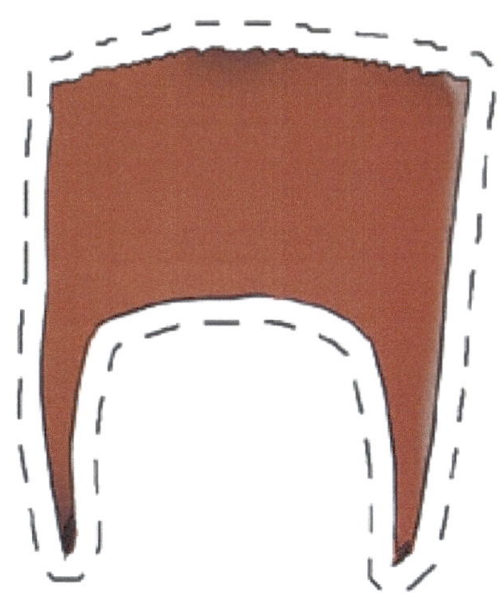

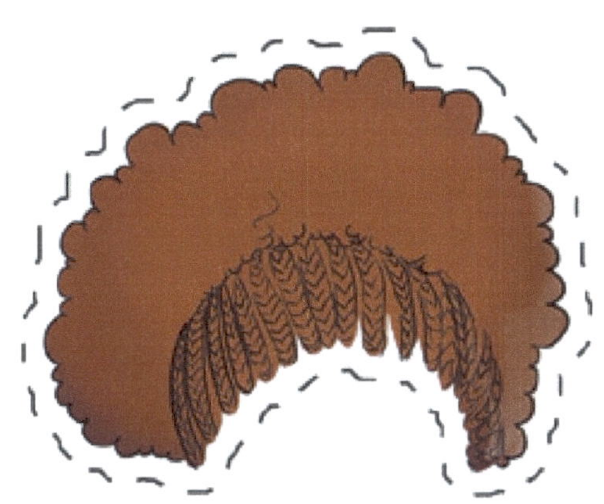

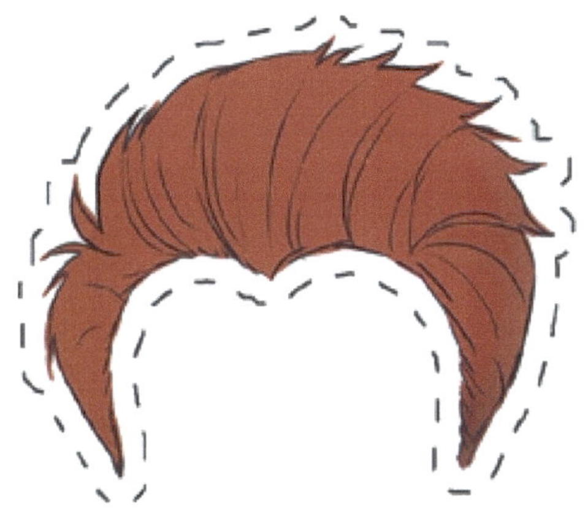

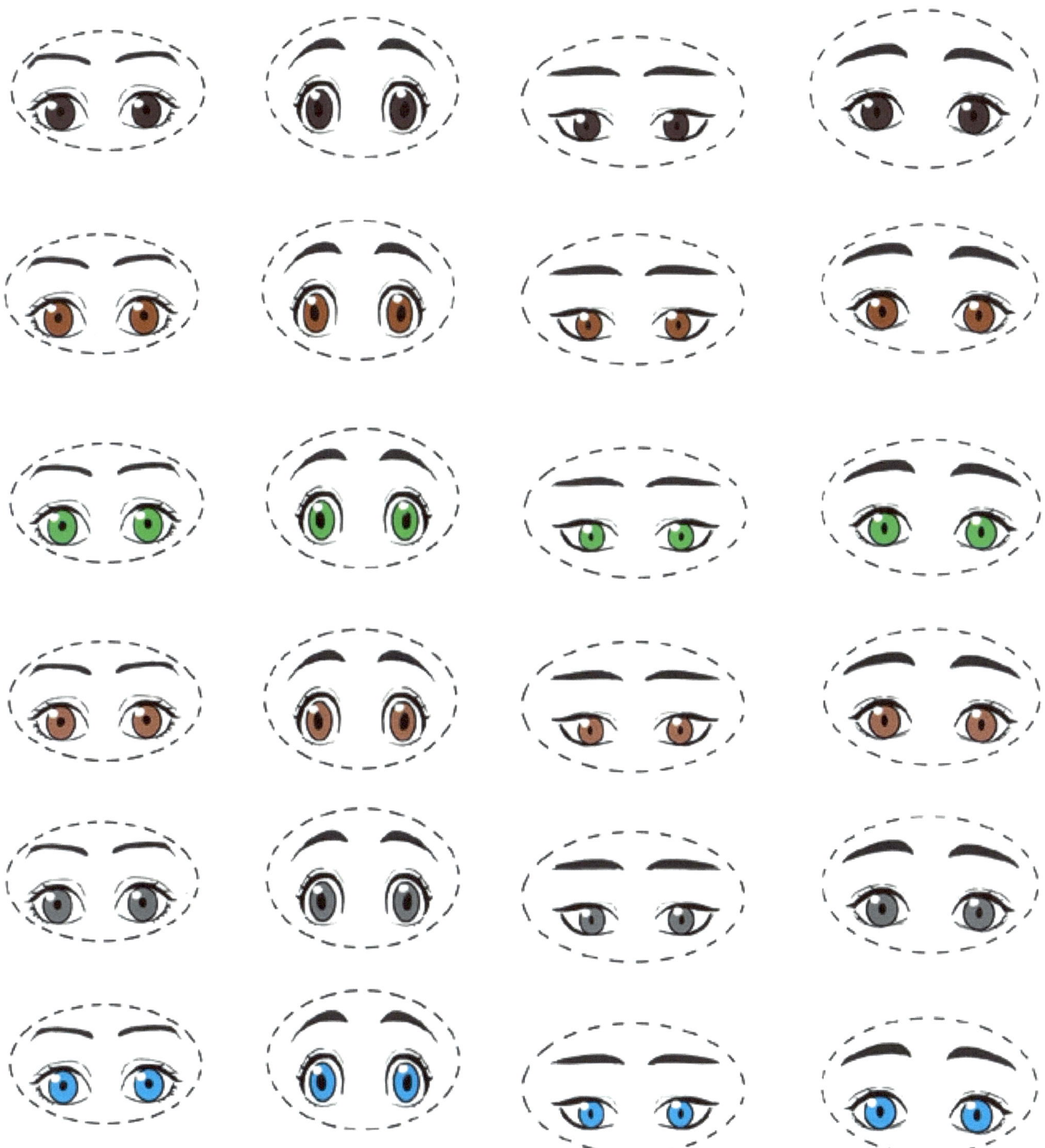

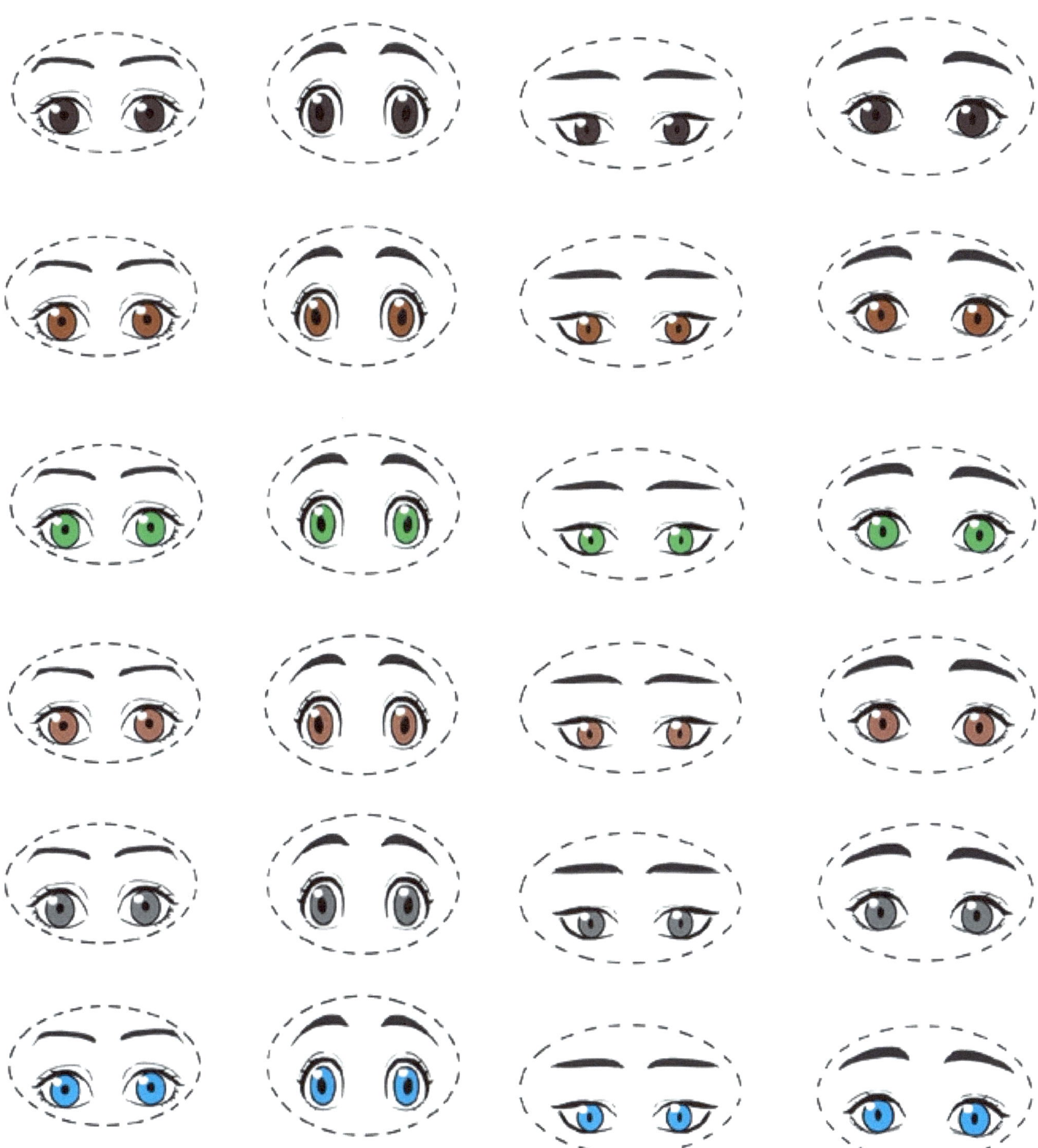

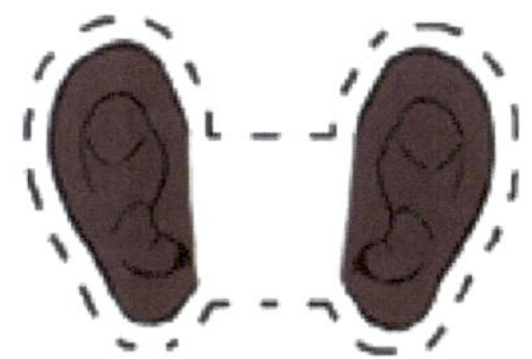
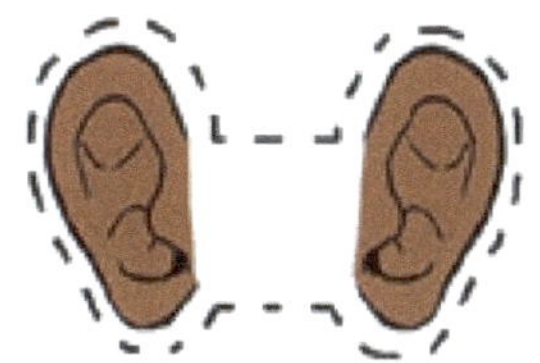
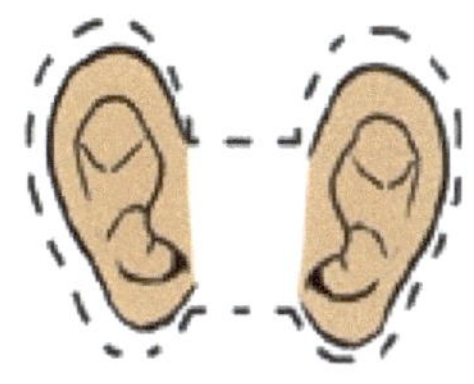
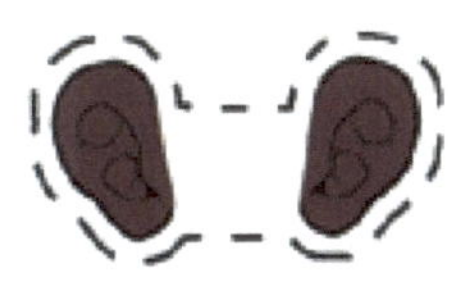
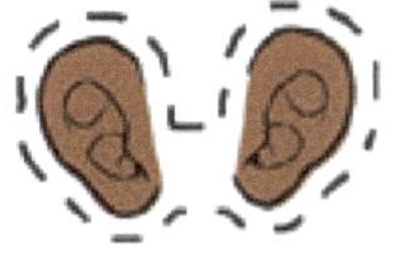
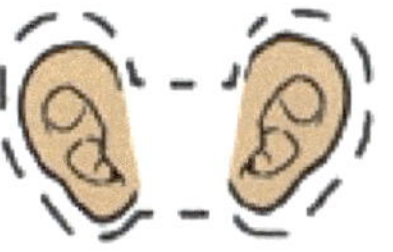
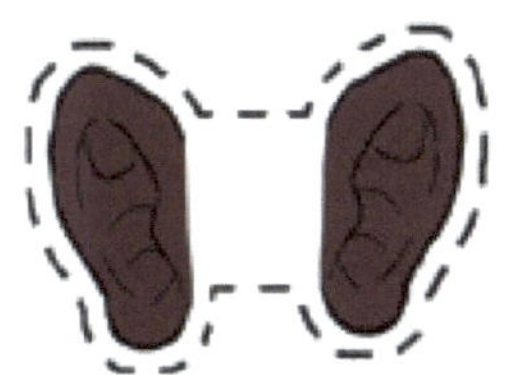
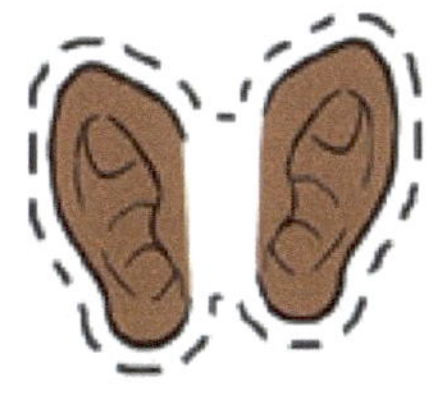
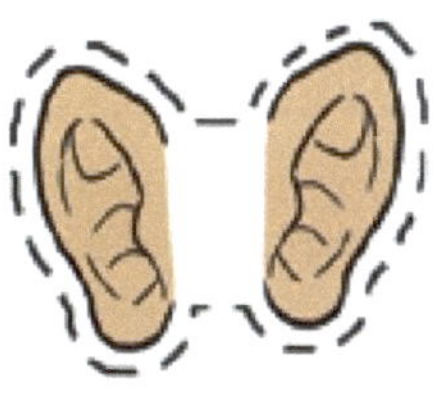
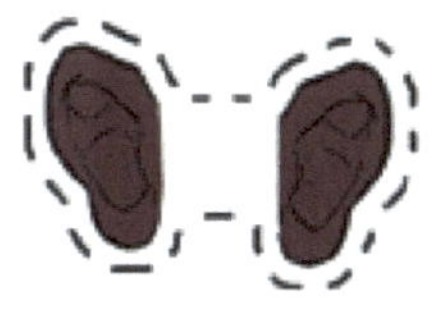
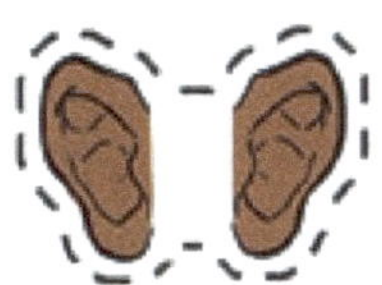
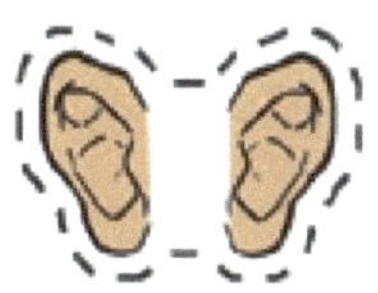

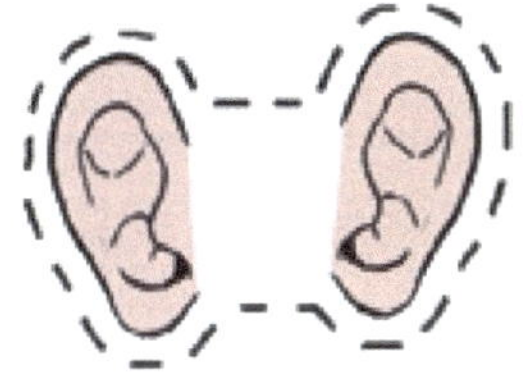
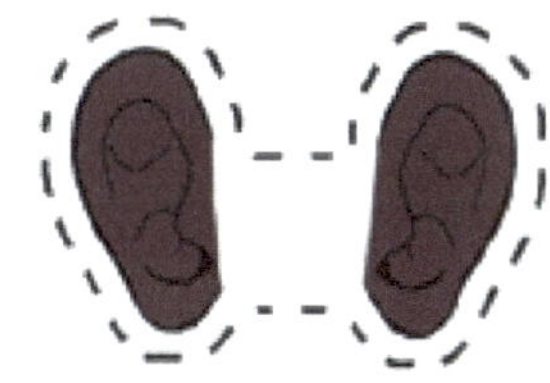
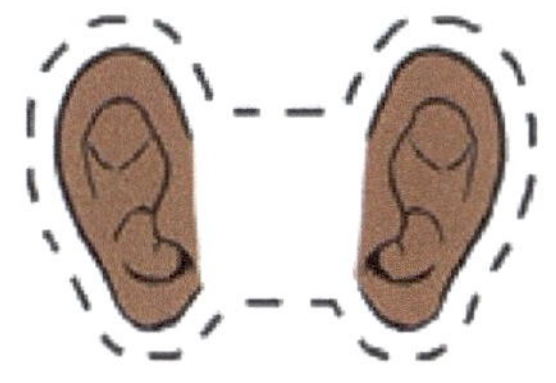
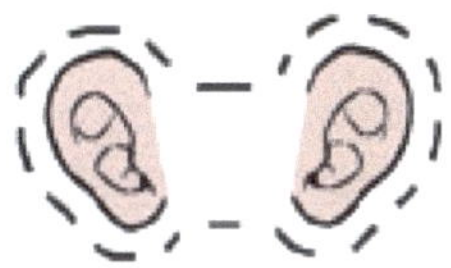
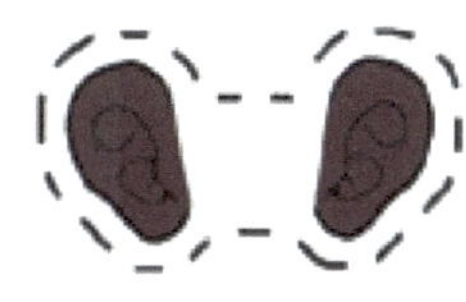
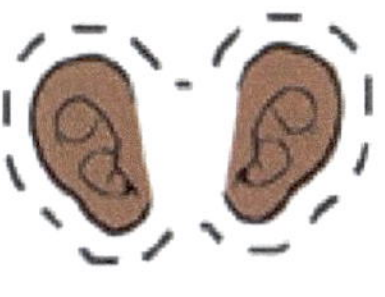
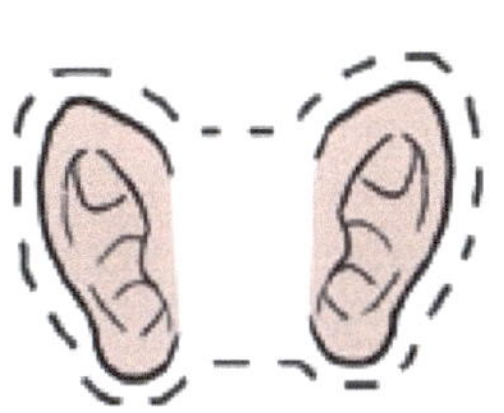
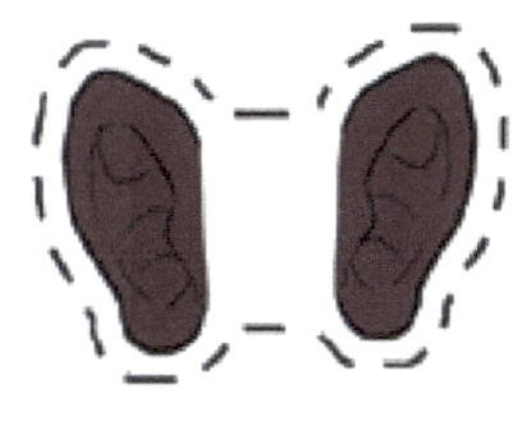
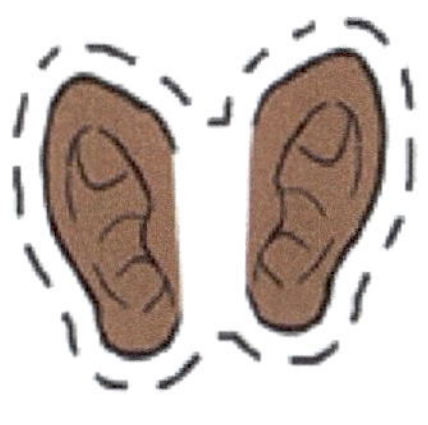
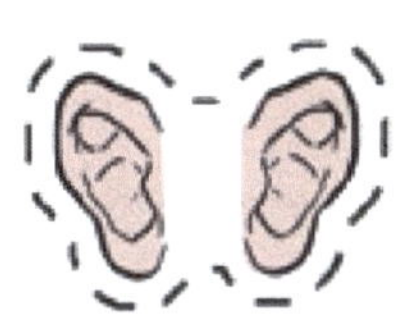
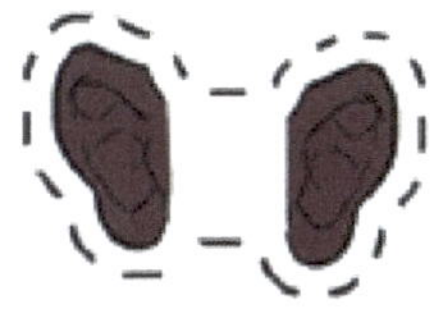
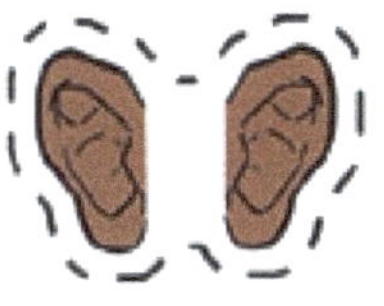

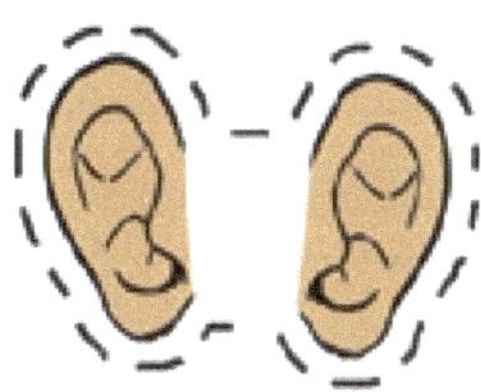

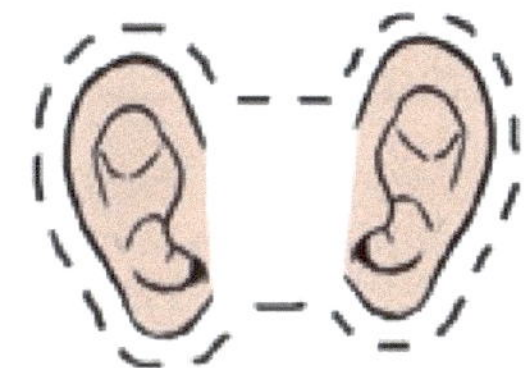

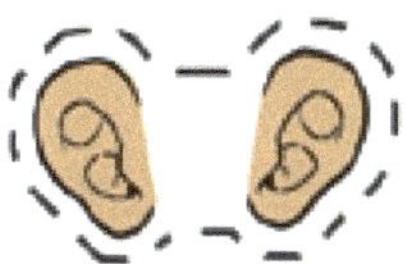

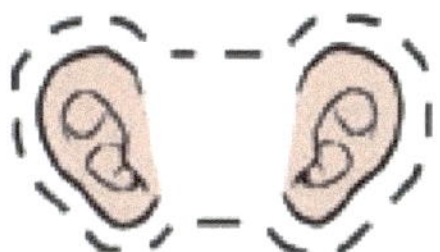

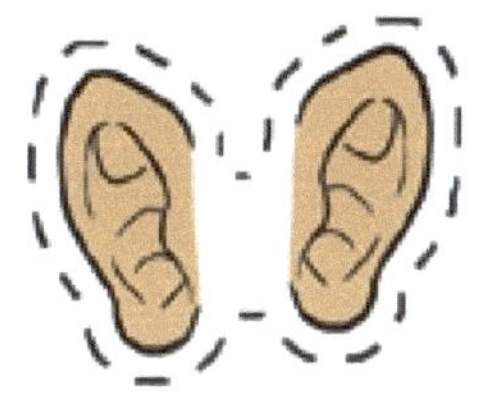

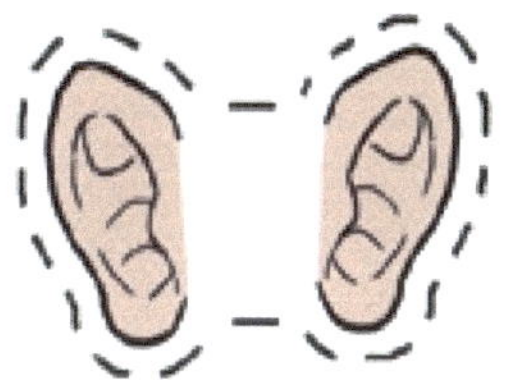

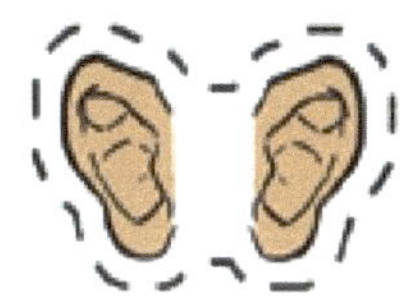

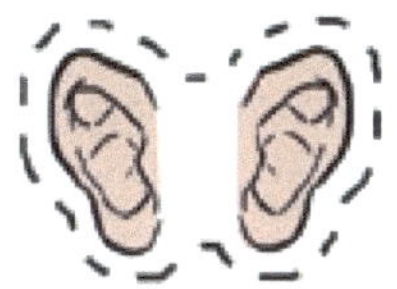

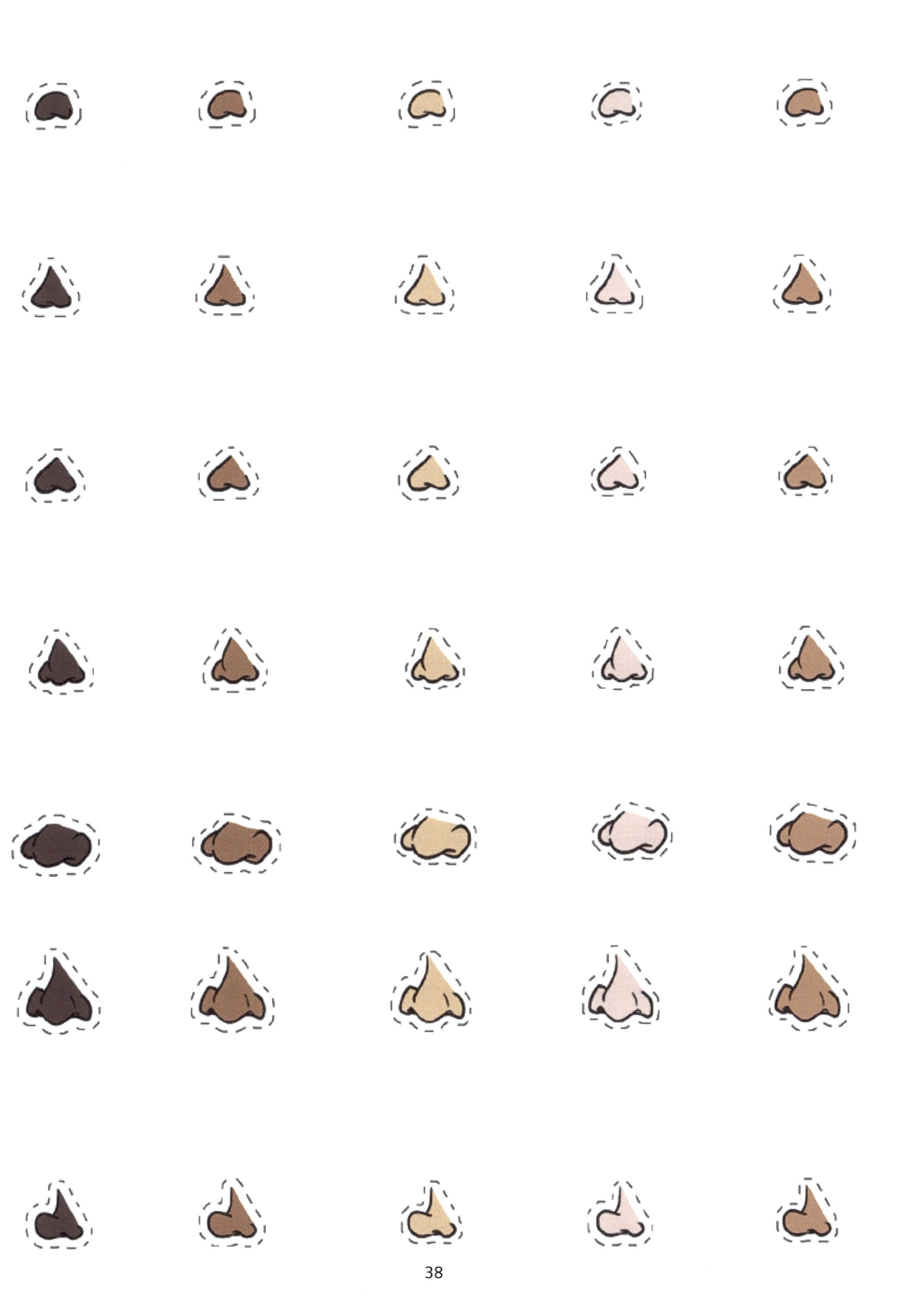

38

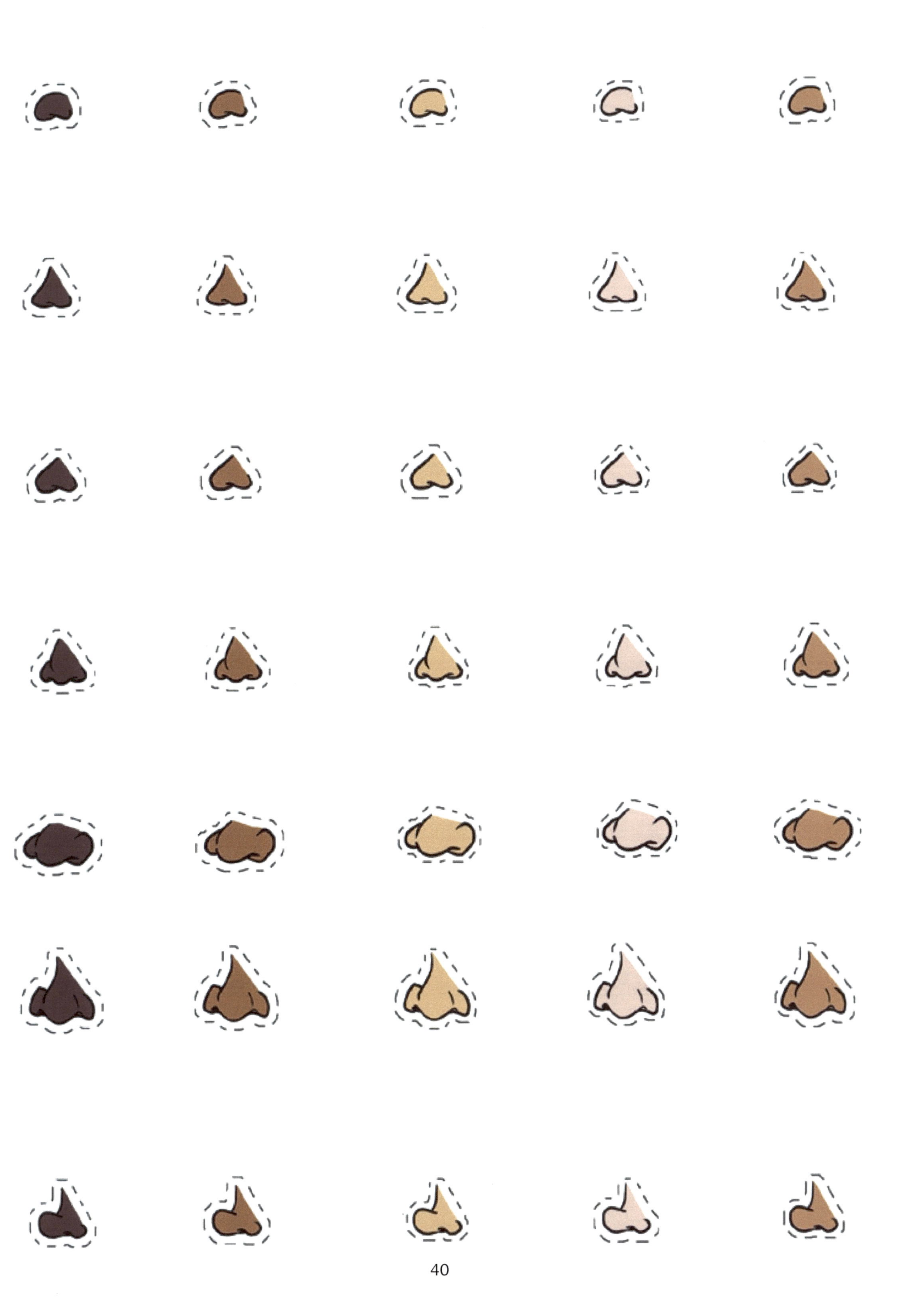

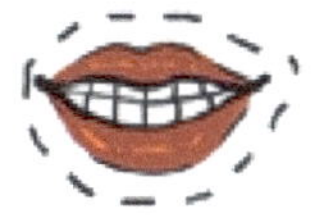
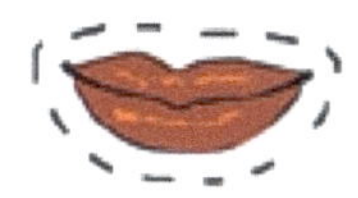
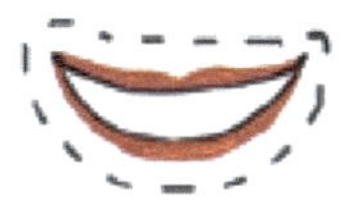
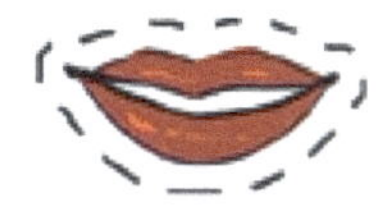
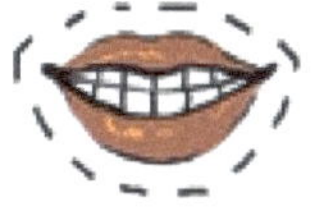
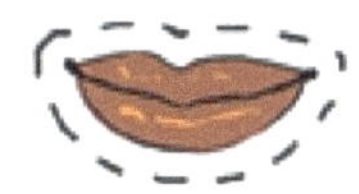
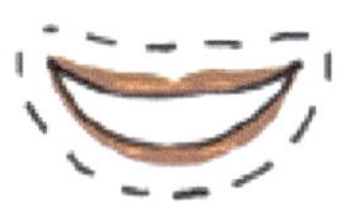
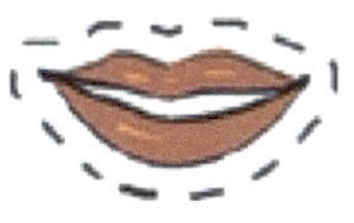
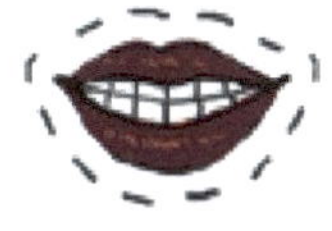
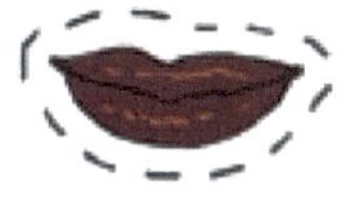
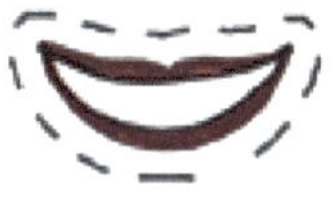
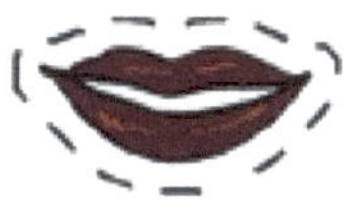
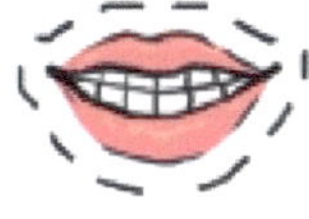
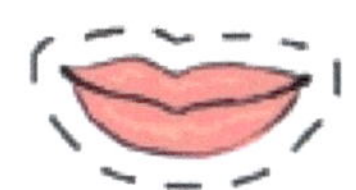
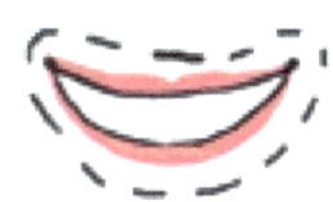
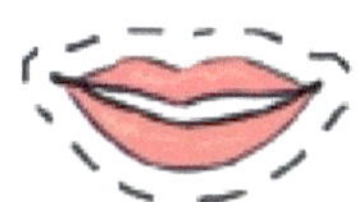

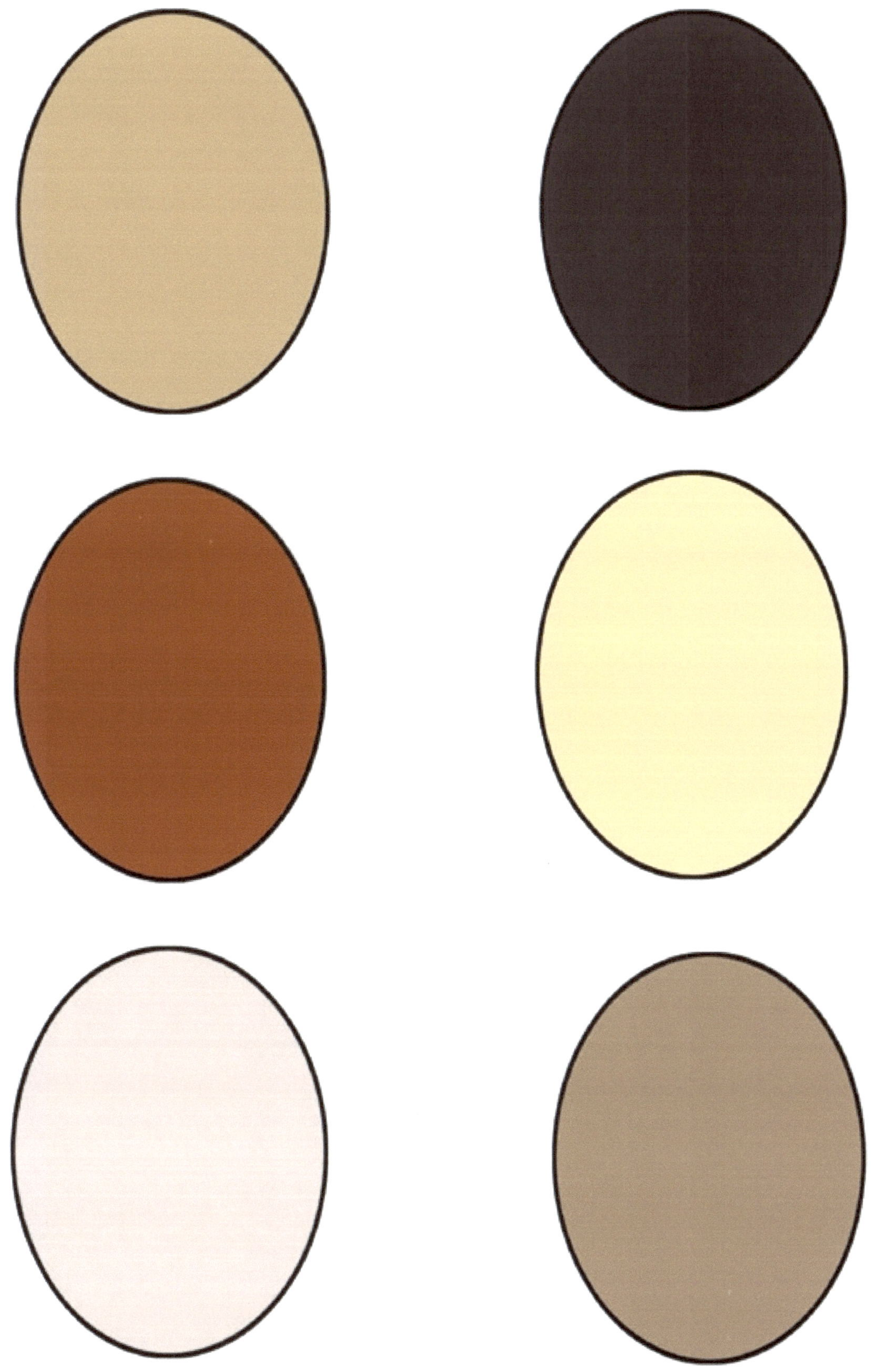

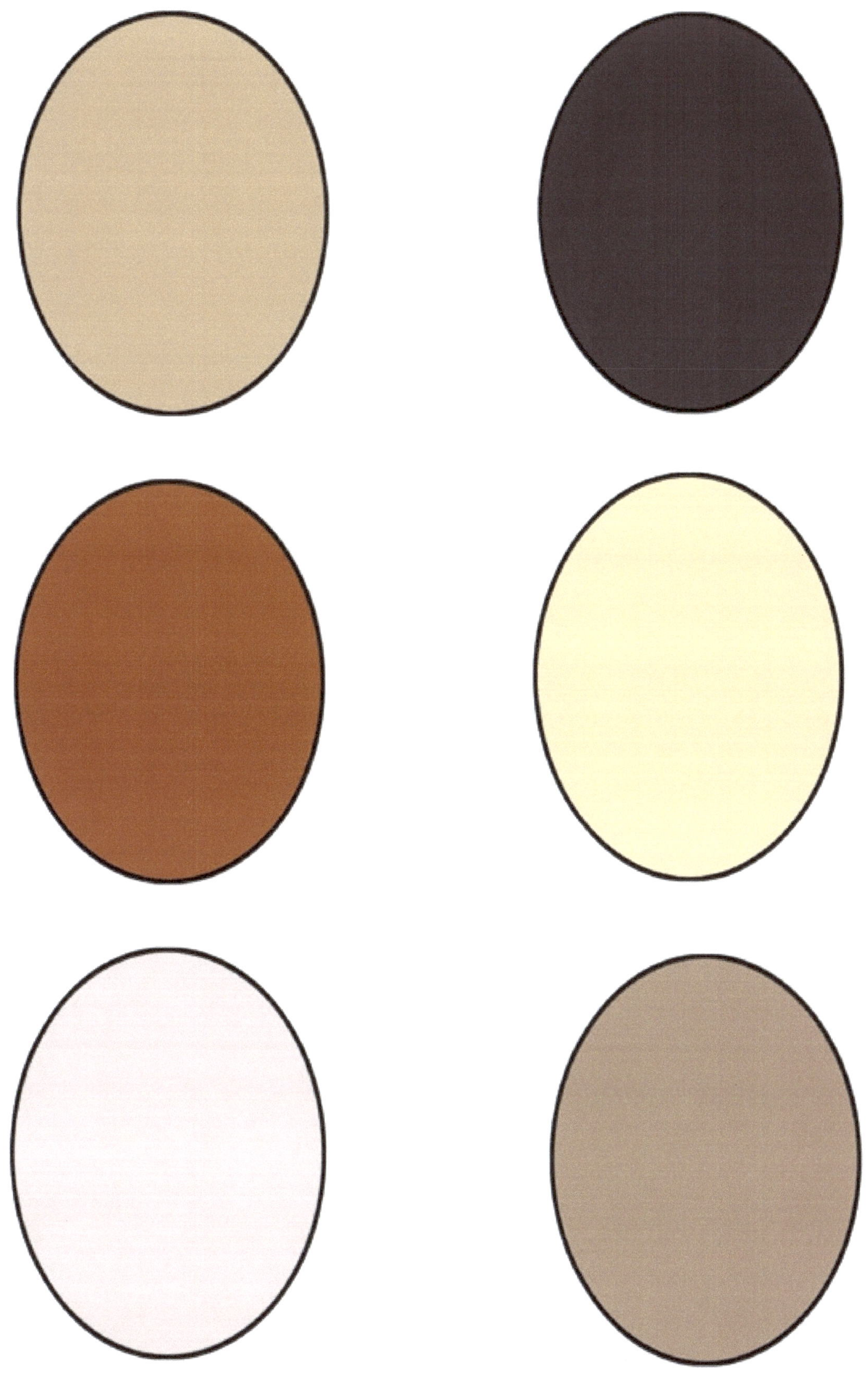

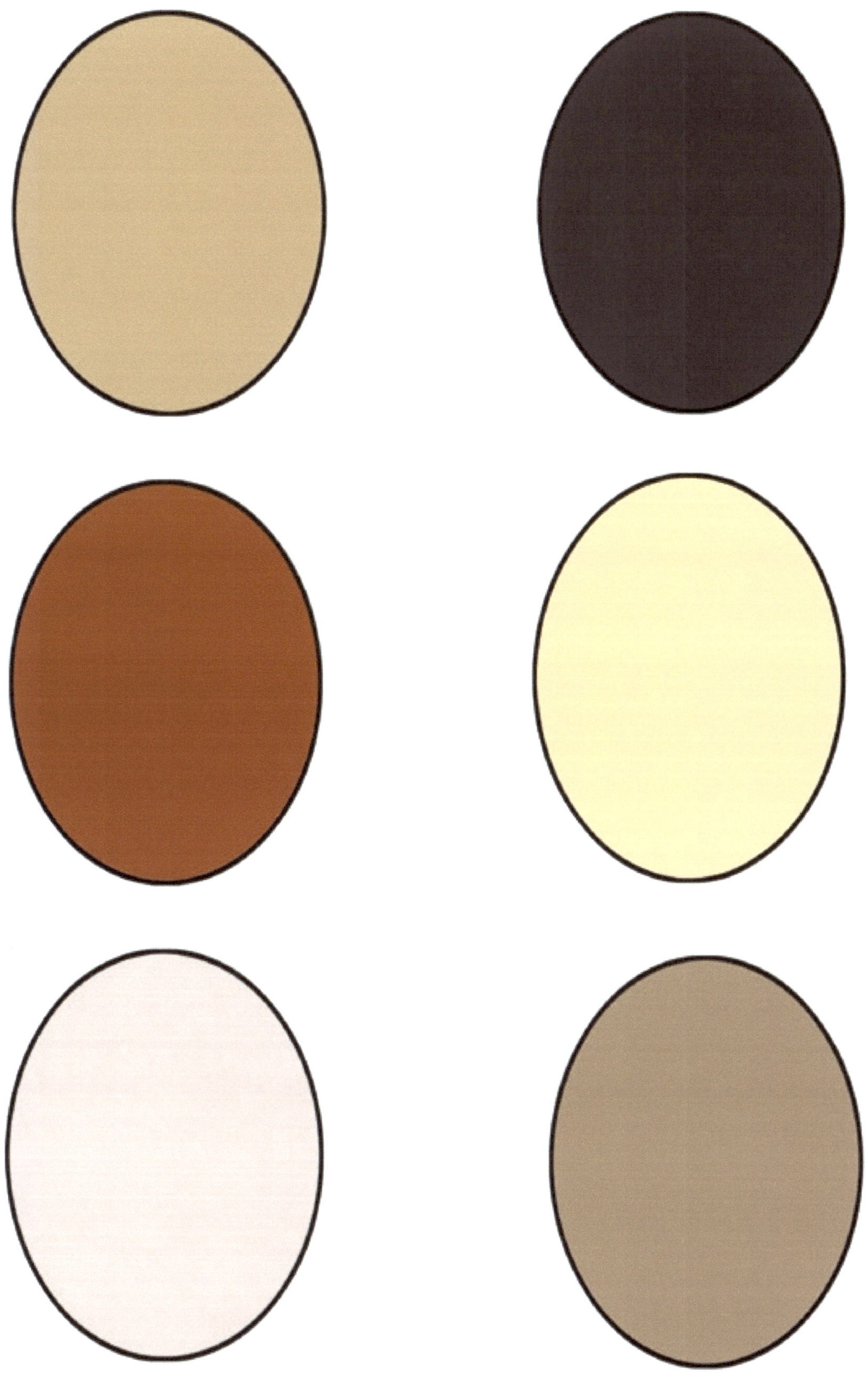